is this the body
        if hovers

The author would like to thank the editors of *Verse*, who first published a chapbook length set of earlier versions of some of the poems under the title "All That Trembles." Additionally, thanks to the editors of *Tupelo Quarterly* for the publication of "They put their mouths up to the heavens, which, by and by brief imaginings, doth take away" and "When in my days I called by," which were accompanied by a very kind introduction by Elizabeth Robinson.

Many thanks to Avery Burns and Joseph Noble for their insight and dedication to the work.

Much affection and thanks to all my dear readers, editors, encouragers, chastizers, and fellow pilgrims: Mom, Dad, Elizabeth, Bill Clevenger, Annie Clevenger, Kate Clevenger, Susanne Dyckman, Megan Pruiett, Laura Walker, Stephen Hemenway, Margie Stein, and Paula Koneazny.

And of course, much love to my dear wife and steadfast editor, Lizzie, who is always the song I love to sing.

Cover photograph "A Dried Leaf II" by Kristina Krause is used gratefully by permission of the artist.

Typesetting and book design by the author, under the gracious guidance and care of Stephen Hemenway.

Text and titling set in Sabon MT.

Published by:
lyric& Press
Avery E.D. Burns, Publisher
San Francisco Bay Area

Distributed by:
Small Press Distribution
1341 Seventh Street
Berkeley, CA 94710-1409
Phone: (510) 524-1668
Email: spd@spdbooks.org
Web Site: www.spdbooks.org

ISBN-10 Number: 1-889098-15-9
ISBN-13 Number: 978-1-889098-15-9

is this the body if hovers

t o d d   m e l i c k e r

lyric& Press

for Margie and Paula

He murmurs day and night, and he shall be like a tree

eat the world's
few, few in

light, light must
consume

feed on thy
spirit, substantial

or fennel'd,
fess'd up

he murmurs
himself,

himself a
tree

favorable be
this wrestle &

into this
wrist & into

this resistance
seek

a narrow due,
all night a

marrow
dew

1 : 1

'twill be a tattered weed

w/
scrutiny

kiss her w/
wheat

& shelter
a

small earth
held

excuse, we
shall dash

them &
shall

sum
them

some thrift-
lessening

fracture

Who's fresh repair, if then

pare, art your
function is

art, your
perception

if you
live

by, i lie
down by

remember'd not
to be as

i slept that
face, or fox,

for should on
your people

wear, your
wasting

Nature's bequest gives nothing, but doth lend

on whetstone
lift up

your light,
thou of

thyself,
set your

heart
on your

body, its
bed

its
lending

library,
give nothing

but traffic
in the

straits,
set me

down, doth
deceive

me safely
& prove me

chase

4 : 4

Though they with winter meet

blood, frost-
fleck'd

nor it
nor

beauty
i lay

effect
before

my voice
before

to make
right

to take
a collection

in the
mouth

expect
winter

& every
bareness

a
choir'd

Be not self-willed for thou art much too

                fair, my
                eye

                is
                worn

                inheritance
                by

                currency
                woke

                by line
                my burial

                i take
                the

                upswum
                bed & its

                kind
                coin-slot

                its fish-
                bone

                body
                in

                bright
                math

Under each eye, each earthly eye

he said
to himself

"i will go
alone w/
you"

& she to
herself

He revealeth, he searches conscience

like a
head

on
fire, lest

a lion
halo'd

highmost
outgroups

noon,
let fly

the arrow,
dwell

under one
eye

one
earth

cuts the
hours

Whose speechless song, being many, seeming one

whose
splendor

a fixed
moon

the fixing
sun

the oxen
have

two different
coloring

eyes, among
them

each
music

each
sad

music,
what moves

order, what
is

adam, his
mutual

string

But beauty's waste hath in the world an end

your window
knows

it's
mortal, i

acclaim
the world

an end
hath your

particles
wasted, truth

partially
wept so,

let me
hymn

let me
wend

your name,
its accustomed

(i promise
you, both

guest &
host)

makeless,
the lower

& lover
as door

9 : 9

His ways are uncertain in every hour

lost in
kind

loosed
from his

hands, the
thought:

a tree loses
its leaves

a theory, too,
expires—

find a roof
only

to ruin it,
find a

song only
to

be done w/
it, a lion's

skull rests
out the

rain in a
culvert

penance,
a coin

w/ his

mind

printed
on it

You could make the world away

in a curl
the word

i swelter,
how

could you
say

shelter decay
like an

arrow shot
through

my narrow
rest, fasten

the moon to
my

face, kill
faster

this bird
startled

brow, for thou
shalt wane

into breath
thou

shalt grow
a cup

to hold

my thread;

its reigning
mask

Then of thy beauty do I question make:
the organ of intention is divided

in her
a heart

of clock,
in him

the antarctic
as seen

from
space

clearly the
counting

is begun,
clever, they

haste the
same

Your sweet issue, your sweet form, eternal cold

no more
mine

than an
oak

mine, or
the oak

possessing
me, turn

my face
to keep

out the
rot, the

throat
roe &

the little
white

glands a
prerequisite

of always
the roots

you
know

are no
longer

yours, none

so

numerical
as these

drowning
lights

or
eyes

And yet methinks I have astronomy

as i derive
my shell,

beauty's
time-lapse

stares from
many

eyes, i
will

see the
coming

of my
felling,

the
yearling

constellation
of my

collar
bravery

Holds in perfection his hat, his hands,
but a little moment

as he
takes

from you,
take from

yourself
broken &

spoked,
for he

travels
by

engrafting
more

& more
sky

onto his
back, first

placing
the

trees upon
his

hands &
fore-

arms
& you,

by

eclipsing

the night
this

self-same
vow

w/in the
wasteful

little
moment

of sun
&

star-meal
met

a
necessary

blood
-orbit

So should the lines of life, that life repair

sweet skull
let your

sweet skill
set the

garden in
rows,

so too,
sorrow

abounds
& the

ground is
drawn

into its
one dawn

line

selah

I take my fill, wide awake of your image

you, the
apple

that has
come

upon my
heart,

the dark
that

is my heart
half-

cut, that
you

should
live twice

& hide w/in
a pale

green
circle—i'm

surgically
awake

w/ metric
seed

Makes my legs like a gazelle's and
stands me on the heights

show me
your

nape, fair
from

fair declined,
the

deer w/
mist

allotted from
her

feet &
heaven

tilted
for your

pleasure, i
was

an eye that
is

a furnace
owning

or a fiery
horn—

where two
waters

rescue, there

amassing

in darkness,
our

density
pines

Make glad and worry seasons as thou fleet'st

burning out
gold, more

world now
& diurnal

our devouring
blemished

whisper, our
sweet

fading
circuit, she

goes out
now

a tall sun
abundant &

once
allowed

An eye more bright than theirs,
but we arose and took heart

the heart
it

took &
a man

in hue,
all eyes,

takes
gently,

enroutes
the trees

of rescue,
more

bright, while
more

she &
he will

have well
looked &

well
acquainted—

a'piety
nightly

So it is not with me as with that withheld

in the hour
of

the shoulder
this

how of the
face

w/out end
your

hand will
find

out your
right

hand turn
louder

& being
traced will

let us
ascend

of the
shoulder

& so w/
rondure

hem
erase

And his lips entreaty you with sun
and moon, with earth

      the flower
      filled

      of being
      bending

      &
      keeping

Presume not on my heart, when mine is slain

tellbline
so

warilous, peri-
lous &

grain, the
brain

waxy &
groundout—

a sleeper
of earth-

limbic, for
he

has done,
for all

that beauty
clay

crown'd
none, & i

counted out
my

bones, they
counted

out a'well
sign

keeper,

presumed

rather, river
thin or

a'thine mine
hands

& feet;
trees, given

Who with his fear is put beside his part

more than
that

more my
life

she more
brings

want
back, a

flitting
speech

the leaf or
after-gill

pursuit

To hear with eyes, belongs as its

book
at least

look, when a
presager

begins,
orion to

oriole—
antipodal

the tidal
ordeal

'my cup
overflows'

Now see what good 'twas eyes, focal

wherethrough
the sun

has borne
myself

on a boat
of beliefs

muted—
mutation

& the
earth has

lifted its
head, its eyes,

for
eyes have

done
&

drawn the
heart

to table,
the heart

at proof

I lift the life-breath, essential-self, empty-handed,
for the keepers of precepts

the stars,
their

fair leaves
spread

to breath,
will

inherit the
rest

& have
ours

And there my eyes at all times to inherit

but as the
marigold favors

from the net
he draws

my feet, keeps me
empty-handed

at the center:
the seed

that glows,
a sun's drowsy

eye grows;
encodes

sieges

Where I may not remove nor be

boreal
guise

bruise
bright

green to
careful

sleeve
& so

grow
amazed

or more
prized

I have walked in my wholeness, shall walk
in my wholeness, shall walk in your youth

burn pure
bare

in wanting
thought

pairs of
harms &

worms go
round

your altar-
word

we're a fair
aspect—

apparel
intelligent,

accordingly
restored

On a rock, he raises me up, and now my head also rises

quiet, limb,
abide the

pilgrimage
by twin

sweetness,
the night

recesses,
whoso

finds your
fear

to draw
near to

Far where I abide, should gather me in

imaginary
thee

night of
the mind

throatful
or thoughtful

do i
ask

by limb
by day

quiet
sight, a

watchful
firmament

Tend them, lift them up for all time, bear them up

worry-shone
the even,

lest the
rock is

mute to
me—

for thwart
the wired

heartward
draws

either, &
thy

guild'st
heat

twined
through,

'o happy
plight'

i've a
tremor

to my
grace

where the
eye

lifts its

sun

& sets
its

pace

And with my song, day by night and night by day

we remember
but

dust &
breath

returned,
or begun

& render when
a far

star cried
&

lit us
out

of its
common

calamity
mouth

So do I tell the day to please him, thou art bright

as
will

a hand
plead

its
wounds

in even
every

tide on
tine

selah

That then I scorn to change my state with kings

a doe
gives

birth,
lays

bare, a
forest

hews
fair, like

the lark,
who

breaks
her

When to sessions of sweet silent thought

when up
out of

the quiet
well-

hid cup
what

flood
-ward

sun &
forehead

stung w/
ash

will
silhouette

& grain
silo

certain

But if the while

lover, the
eyes are

exchanged
& rings

extrapolate
the

moment
of entry;

how like
a diver

longer or
longer

And thou, all they, hast all the all of me

i am
lost, least

to the
point

i don't
look for

myself,
to the eye

wearing to
texture

blind, smooth
my throat

& belly,
the

vessels
many &

icon'd—
wide-opened

w/
casualties

That due of many, now is thine alone—
my eye is worn out, my throat

eye of
white or

blind
obsequial

night makes
virtue

how vex'd
at my

throat &
religion

so steals
the thin

vertical
lines:

once
forgiven

the statue
brings life

to
life

For this every faithful one prays to you in time of need

when i was
silent,

when the
the water

approached
you,

you found your
way to it

on the backs
of roaring

rocks, as one
decreased in

a sum, as
one

outstripped—
you appeared

to me as a
young

song

Vouchsafe me but this

my head

in heel,

hand in

meal, a

council

in my

eye &

tree to

celebrate,

adore i

new

into

tongues

Suns of the world may stain
when heaven's suns staineth

    & she spoke
    out of

    an eye, a
    sovereign

    eye, one
    breath

    from her
    eye kissed

    mine & mine
    it became

    the heaviest
    sun, the

    devastating
    pursuit—

    my crescendo
    heart

And by the breath of his mouth all their array

as long as
the sun

& i feel
it upon

me, the
sky is

wilderness

Was but one hour mine

look out
of

the true
at me

& see
me whole

& burning
the sky

so cold
crushed

as to
never

catch
blue

All men make faults, and certainly I in this

take care
of every

bone, sweet
thief

& lack no
good, for

i lie
down

on your
hunger

& await
the

blaze-light
of your

face to
wake

me

So may my own prayer come back to my breath

take my
part;

a beautiful
day

is not
enough to

give physic
to my

messenger
bone, the

cloud thou
break

&
sing-by

And their faces were no longer shadowed

for sometime
sun, now

sometime
scar, for

sometime
weighed,

now some-
time water,

vibrant

In your light, we seed light, seam light

abyss, thy
light

& love
undivided

are the
same,

twain my
shelter

into wing
&

confession's
bright need

And she caressed him with her eyes

bright animal,
confess

to me
thy shelter,

though it alter
not your

lingering
abyss, nor

bring not
your

binding
sight, still

might i
sing &

still will i
sky

until i am
one, made

two
denied

Though I fall, I will not be flung down,
that I, in thy abundance, am sufficed

whether
every

white
swallow

or throat
will

word me
i don't

know, only
the

supple
now,

only the
quick as

the
grass

*And she that calls on thee, let her
bring forth eternal numbers*

after
consciousess

this is how
i know

i will leap
to

the earth:
from

days to
fill a

circle,
a circle

inside
a bell,

& the
freefall

begins
headfirst

Dost give invention light, mine argument

call to
mind

your
arrows

of your
arrow'd

mind, the
outlier

fulfilled,
an

accelerating
embrace

Behold, thou hast made my days
a handbreadth, a hand's breath

what stranger
is

a stranger
w/ you

eukaryotic
sorrow & my

farther, my
sparrow

a measuring
leave

or traveler's
guest, the

sun inside my
cell, my cells

In my thought a fire burned. I spoke with my tongue.

> my heart
> hot
>
> stemmed not
> &
>
> sweet
> consumed
>
> strewn

Take all my loves, my love, yea, take them all, severity

w/ increasing
leasting

he bent
towards

me &
put

a quarter
in my

mouth—
this is

'not a
song'

slanted
to overtake

the
mechanized

bone or
brazen

Everlasting and everlasting, amen and amen,
I am concealed in my heart

    & i am coiled
like a

scroll to
your writing,

sometime
absent

your some-
time

two-fold
riot

soil, per-
missive

in my
song

a new
mouth

When hast thou then more than thou has before

we strung
novice

between us
&

squared
the stone

mark on
our

back, our
favor

carried
well-spring

to
last

Beauteous thou art, therefore to be assailed

the too
many

lie of
this

valv'd
existence:

tomorrow
&

tomorrow
an iron

heart
made

from a
ship's

stolen
iron

And yet it may be, the doe longs

i bend my
night

will bend
my

loss,
animal,

the neck
is thirst
.

& song
offens'd

Both find each other, and I, my whole being thirsts

for an un-
known

deer whose
plant

memory
is a tree

on its skull,
an oak

from
the bricks

of its own
animal

mind-after-
death: will

my sky
turn a

culpable
climbed

anthem
when assured

we meet
in pulp

as pulp

messiah'd

&
branching

reach

How bent my being, I am on my way to the wonderful

lay down
the

neck of
the doe,

the neck
of the

abyss,
softly

i lean
into the

water, my
breath

nearly

selah

All days are nights of the sea till I see thee

tabernacle,
who is

the dark, the
bright

dark
shoulder

occupied
until

further we
mend,

meant
curled

unto light
sent of

a dark
pinlock

—we
we've

So much have earth and of water wrought

stay upon
the stray

farthest
thought, for

i am not
thought, i—

my heart
has not

slipped back,
though

the elements
follow

from limits,
your right

hand & your
arm—the light

of your face
that raises

the secret
removes, the

hill that
hides

the sun,
the one

that takes

my days, my

praise
fraught

thru

My life being made of four, with two alone,
these present-absent

messenger
whenever

messenger
when, rain

meant
returned

when
othered, my

desire in the
needle-

work, swift
the

other two,
another

thee

For every person, I grow every antler, gazelle

its hair is
standing on;

his hair is
standing

on end,
it bows his

head, he
crosses its

feet; people
& oxen both

have hooves—
the living

will guide
the dead to

death
& the dead

hold out
their

horns, we've
one long

& one
thinned

line

Fear not when the continents drift apart, as a moon

last me
after me

the eye
that

splits the
atom

the blue
eye, its

thievery
attendant

the earth
the iris

one white
favor &

the famous
book of

accidents—
one swimmer's

eye open
in your

solar system
chest

trapeze net
or nest

Mine eye, mine heart, I loom upon the earth

delicate
desolate

in the
hip-socket

the earth
removed:

i hung
upon,

around the
loom

the jacob
or joshua

tree

An inquest of thoughts, the clear eye's moiety

many handled
stag

many limbed &
many &

wheeled, the
armor of

love is
moveable

scaled,
the

head has
uplift, has

the arc—i am
variegated, a

certain
halo

chart

Within the gentle closure

he has gone,
she has

gone up
transverberate

as will the
pulley &

barter, a mind
thrown

back, by every
neck, no

further, the
mouth is

the only eye
to bind

our copper
burden or

gaping
blindfold

Thence thou wilt be stol'n, I fear, so night

lay home
& im-

part,
the animal

lays itself
down

next to
the

arrow; your
clock

consumes
me—&

i love
your

clockworks

I will open my dark saying upon the harp, thine eye

gravity's
allegiance

& on that mouth
that sun

i show
favor

& wear out
in my image

after
her, there

where the
neck is

mute to
me

Against that time, if ever that time come

that's if there's
a deer

in the
roots

& a tree
to grow

out of
my collision:

hide or
habitat, so

we are
hidden,

falling thru
an aortic

overlay to
which heaves

fire on fire,
abdicating

a will
w/ mineral

adjustment—
such names

to call
upon the

earth

I know all the birds of the mountains, and
the wild beasts of the field are mine

utter sun
utmost

& rising
flame

in the
mouth, burnt

in the
craw (for i

have not
told

you, if i
hungered)

a covenant
devours,

delivers
new: the

wordless
grain,

the horse
that

bears
me true

further
to speed

&
spoil

In wingéd speed no motion shall I know

wash me
w/ snow

wash me
w/ bone

wash me
still wiser

& wash me
to song

thoroughly
wronged

&
crow'd

In what is concealed, make wisdom,
from where thou art

the hidden
part

haste me
hence

in
aspersion

or broken
delivery

a fiery
snow

a flesh
startled

the hyssop
grows

near
walls

& against
lips

Go as the time that keeps you at my chest

commonary
it teeters

the seldom
tree, gripping

inside my
seldom

house, a
solemn living

lung
redaction

intent; the
sun w/

its
choices

The which will not ev'ry hour survey, new unfolding

        nest couples,
        first

        put on a
        thirst for

        flame &
        subscription,

        circumnavigate
        the neighborhood

        sun-biter, brighter
        in bearing

        your heart-
        sun, some

        many handed
        strand to be

        hunted, latched
        to hope

        or roof
        before

Since seldom coming in the long year set,
like an olive tree, whose blesséd key

three-in-one

prometheus

my bearing

my glorywork

in reach

& in thy

blame

But you like none, none you, for constant heart

these
star assemblies

discerning,
falling as someone

seeking your
million

substances, whereof
& sorely

scattered might
restore;

might fable
in a

brought
knock

Speak of the spring and foison of the year,
what is your substance and stranger

there is
none, my

fascicle, who
friends to

bone &
makes not

my scout, a
fear

tenderful—
the counterfeit

meteor should,
my poison,

discern the
shadow you

split
into

But for their virtue, only is their show

from every
eye, you

are about
to

help me—so
are not

they
hiding

among
me &

tinctured
brightly

for to
sooth, true

Look, I would wander far away and lodge in
the wilderness's throat, would haste to
the streaming wind and the storm

measure

morning

evening &

noon:

the work

of

unswept

stone

to root

selah

Which but to-day by feeling allay'd,
the muted dove of distant places

else call it
winter, my

fishhook,
my love; be

thou & be
of my

vows un-
counted

in part, the
shore

in flesh
& valve

involving
a cloud

although

My heart is fixed, o god, my heart is fixed

the earth is
fixed awake, the

eye is fixed w/
orbit, swallowed

by the watchtree,
the watch-

face, a fixing
point, the flown

is fixed & spent,
while the moon

burns a hole
in the hour, in my

sovereign bone,
lion, road,

the dawn is
crashing

down, her
neck

flexed

And patience, tame to difference, bide each check

just your
hands

he will
remove—

be where
you list

& lie,
linger

to be
weighed

Before your fingers can feel the thorns, he will
take them away in the whirlwind

the neck
to suffer, beckon

the hand
an hour

to crave
your

charter, your
earth

your freely
understood

bramble: a
ladder propped

on the terrace
moon

to
trade

Whether we are mended, or whether better they
to this composed course of your thought

five-hundred
corners

of your
sun

hunger
wonderment

& the
night

delivering
invention

or its
first

diameter

Time doth transfix the flourish set on youth,
delves the parallels

i shall
measure

you, washbasin,
a broken

astonishment
or brow

of salt, how
was i

brought into
the city

by wave &
quell; this

cracked
eclipse &

well-feathered
scythe

Is it thy will thy image should keep open

mock-up
day

mocking-
bird, how

my earth
is

heavy, while
i made

my home
in an erst-

hidden
kingdom &

liking your
elsewhere

sake,
jealous

this fossil
singing

stood

If they be laid in balances, no shape so true,
no truth of such account

brood bowing
well & a

remedy
man

a balance-scale
w/ my

every
tongue,

there are
two, they

are
lighter

unhanded
&

breath-
handed, dark

departed
hewn,

home

I behold you weary land, weary lamb,
in the night-watches I dwelt with you

so too, in the
sanctum, so

greenly in her
& vanished,

a vanishing
lineal, a

plunge posits
scavenger

memory, the
crush for

portion, &
she in them

served to
foxes

And in them, still green, life

canst thou
filament

filigree
champion

agree to an
extent of

salt then
century

vessel
to the

secret
-éd twist

That kingdom will come and take my sea,
my arrow shot away

the kingdom of the
shore, & deep

is the heart or
outworn, or buried

should the eye-
eternal, the

ocean grain,
the inward thought

of every arrow-
worker come:

to pull out their
own

tongue, pull
out your

own plea

You ready their refrain, for so you ready it

flesh shall come
& into you

all flesh decay,
bandless

& since
glass, the

seams were
breath-paid—

startler, it was,
ever warbler

Whose action is stronger than a flower,
they shout for joy, they even sing

black inked
love, blink

& brass'd
eternal, nor

earth, they
even, nor stone

to you
silence is

praise &
into the far-

flung wreckful
gladdened

staid, i went

And art made tongue-flamed by authority

all the
earth

bows,
holdeth

forthsworn,
& thou

tried
as silver

tried,
terrible—

perfect in
risework or

flood-on-
foot, the

miscalled
now mis-

caller
falling

God, even our own god, through

to know
his

earth, her
shine

his lace,
her

rush in
hue

barely the
fearful

yield, a
full-

throated
run

In him whose holy antique hours are given,
the heavens too, poured down before them

another
green,

why do
you

leap,
mountain,

what
do you

count,
beast-of-

the-reed,
please

keep
counting, field,

three
three &

inlaid
three

selah

The solve is this, that thou dost grow taken

the world's
eye for a

matchstick
maker, all

tongues
believed to

the knife-
box,

song-oxen
better than

hooves
have swept me

to haven't—
meet at the

neck, never
to

river nor
thatch

a décor
captive, bracken

in break
a messenger

to send

Let them be turned back for a reward, sweet defect

a kingdom
crow, thou

alone king-
dom outcome

make no
tarry, sweet

out-
numbered

ways,
thy one

for sorrow
two

for illinois,
the illusion of

old men on
magpie

feet, first
letting given

then giving
go, thee

for a girl:
a hanging, cas-

cading tender
boy

Do not go much as with my name rehearse rescue

                i know not
                numbers, as

                i was to
                the many

                heights
                perhaps long

                wearing
                wonders, a

                day-boy,
                the dwelling

                hand that
                writ it

                clay
                too

My tongue too, all fled

recount
horn &

learn
charm,

murmur
the world:

yours
wed &

webbed when
you brought

me
out

As long as the sun, that is, as long as the moon,
which is as long as the sun

they buried
a moon

in my
body, the

long moon
lain still—

may the
seed

of the moon
rustle

like a name
will

forget
me quiet

&
quite

& the
mountain

They put their mouths up to the heavens, which,
by and by brief imaginings, doth take away

my mouth
pressed to

innocence, my
mouth

pressed to
heaven

or none
or

few, a cold
washed ash

could a
cold choir

wash in
fire—

the palm
of my

tongue walks
through

the earth, spills
from leaves

as could they
encase

The earth can have but earth, which is its due

yours is
the winter

boundary, also
yours

the split
ardor who

laid down,
who

perpetually
rises in

dove
decay

(trees to
consequence)

the better
part

a'habit
me

As one brings down from above

axe &
earth

a very
desert very

lain &
yielded

signs as
signs

as antlers
came

as antlers'
son

In tangle of trees or mouthéd memory

in axis song

guilt, held

And not from the desert is one lifted up, deafening

clean to
the straw

attend on
your throat

your name is
near, apple,

palm, prow,
crown, anon

in doubt,
pursuit of

in telling
feign, find

squall

Possessing or pursuing

crow all
wood

'food to
life'

a'stealing
touch

might be,
maybe

neighbor'd
to hide &

hood

So all my best is dressing old words new

       their
       fell

       invention
       sun

       stunned
       animal

       losses,
       still i

       write, i'm
       told

       make
       vows, one

       chariot
       variate

       so null
       grows

       knoll

On the sea was your eye and was not silent

wonder
old, my

hand still
flows, shall

a skull bring
leaf—the

waters, they
saw you, o

god, the
waters

the vacant
wheel

enclosing
knowable

fiery
yellows

to
thread

Let me open my mouth, so oft have I invoked

skinned his
knee, sanctuary

his window,
cicada, will

he ready,
will he

labor to
have added

the amber,
every

fair
dispersed

wintering
husk

or oak or
mercurine

hawk to
crook

And he caught the skies above, and the doors

& under
tree

split
open &

under
thee

surgery
& the deer's

ransom
we island

we isolate
our

careful
ceaseless

And they could not find their hands

swarm of her
arms

swum of her
arms

Quickly may your mercies overtake us
and that stolen word

flesh of
earthen

unbind &
blood—

my sick-in-
love

alone
aids, wearing

number into
number, placing

quay again
the rib,

these stam-
mer'd woods,

the clayed
virtues

The mountains were carried, the mighty cedars ride

bright route
to the

face, worth-
wright, then

extend the
bows wrack'd of

the boat, the
boy, man

& body to
freight

the sea, take
to yourself

a soundless
bread

there is no
nest

nor root
having

Forgotten, the earth can yield me, gentle, when
all the breathers of this world are torn

the moon begins
to cover

itself, the
earth

is made of
breath, i

would feed
you breath

& shoulder,
i would

deliver you
language &

burden, i will
rehearse

the moon,
i will

open my
mouth wide

i will—make
me into a

measure &
i will fill

these into
wheat, you

Divis'd and do so love, indeed like a word

the pines
are

out of
starry

-course, unable
& adam

lend me
your gasp or

prairie, like
one of the

princes, fall
like

a god,
confess

(grasp)

In true plain words, o'erlook in true-plain-telling

rid them
out of

the hand
of balance

brief, this
limit

crease, able
cored

to bird

two birds

And therefore I have slept in your report

high

alone

thistle

hive

this

silence

for a

bulb,

fin, the

wheel

that

burns

down

forests,

seas,

we

take

hold of

which

shall

be

at most

at

make

The barren tender of a poet's debt

like bled

grass,

like straw

pulls a

worthy

out of

of my

socket

chest,

extant, an

ignition

guess

My heart and my flesh, and the swallow a nest for itself

we push back the sleeves
on our cloak of gulls

we rinse the circle
of the cup-face

the day, the early
ever, we

choose shale, choose
plum

delve the better
thousand, a

gentle harm

selah

Then others, for the breath of words respect, withdraw

lay aside
weather or

beside
tongue-twined

the limestone
shall

spring up
a handful of

provens, earth-
forth toward

a spelling of
string, backbones—

perhaps you
could

convince me
on the way

Then I lacked matter, a moon, a shoal

my very
trees, compeer

unceasing
creature, weave

the hurt-work, the
brain & lung

lent countenance
to fruit

mortal more
the interspersals

nucleotidal &
sun-skipped

rot to
gull

And so my patent back again is swerving,
white shocking, deserving

counting
mountains

writeth
deer

she was
born a

lull in
aspen

he, a
stave

to ash,
the

yearfire
enumerates

paper,
folds a

possess-
ive

holy
won't

They surround me like wonders all day long,
they encircle me completely

double-vantage
for light-bending

oblivion, yield
the net

was cast &
i lay

well-acquainted
away, an

obvious water
& a

circle ache
mud-caking the

little squirming
suns, the

divining of
fished eyes

finished
eyes

And his mouth like the sun before me,
the north and the south

tongue among
crowns, songs

the words
crowd, put

a hand to
sea, scour

the hand
to sun

some witness
lover,

a halted
brilliance

hovers, covers
the world

& its
fullness

faults

If thou wilt leave me, do not leave me last

murmured
in white

morrow
grass

a while
world is

a whole
earth is

swallowed
swiftly to

sleep—
the tendrils

of
breath

on our
lips

on our
hands, as

we fly
off

eve &
ever

let

All this away and this me most

messenger
some

measure
some

shelter
some

stalk
some

hawk
for

skill
i will

when
so

may'st
you

With pinion she shelters, with length of days

      lest
      day

      bruise
      alone at

      length,
      make

      palms &
      horses

      quiet
      handles

      bite

Do thy worst to steal thyself away,
and spring up like the grass

vex
upon

bless
to

tell &
night

& the
wild

oxen
blot

now my
rock, all

no
wrong

know

Of life thou art assuréd mine,
and thy life of hands I sing

        sea-floor
        to

        sediment
        &

        climbing
        to

        land, my
        love

        of the
        housing,

        my
        carol of

        cairn &
        benevolent

        least to
        husk

So shall I live, supporting thou are true, thou have voice

thine
thin

line of
fog

clothed &
thought

clothed w/
red-wing

blackbird
workings, the

floods
have

lifted &
the

floods have
lift

you tell
me

shining me
cold

Heaven hurt, and will do none, the temptation slow

i almost
& summer

how long
the

astronomer
i would

have mere
or worn, who

breathes
the eye will

they not
lend a

coarse
pasture

The err in the earth, not known my eye,
not naming thy name

whose
hands

try, kingdom
tongue,

fair to
kind

hill & rest
arrested, here

veil, thy
colliding

name,
chronic they

grow
in stranger

t'morrow, a
chronicle

Hers is the sea and hers made it, for
their habitation chose out thee

crown of
fire, scale

of fire,
crane in

brainfire
fellows

& obey, he
made

bough, he
made brick,

he made
sentient

lent

To truths translated, and for true things deem'd

field to
fault &

fault to
forest

sing, your
errors

could in
tender salt

drift & court,
these woods

willing, be-
come the grass

to lead
me, thou

to breathe me
away

mete
or

vast

And pleasures wait on thee, and thou away

winter
how
like

a writer
nearer
wax

the
pale
bearing

the
blue
muted

leaves
&
their

hands
on
our

mouth
as
it looks

to
the
very

Drawn after you, you pattern of all those

hath been everything,
every hue ab-

sent pied, every
hand lays &

his holy
arm, drawn

his horn, his wing
hath, holy

therein after
sing, hath

holy after
wrong

For wonders done have I been absent in the spring

& his holy arm
& her holy assured

& his holy every
& her holy drawn

& his holy lure
& her holy wrong

in their holy hue, they
grew dress'd

& the vermillion
hung, cutting

In everything, but sweet, but figures

crease in
key into

keen the
small

bird
burn'd

burning
pluck

took

If not from my love's breath, thief

the rain
steals, one

another threshing
shame, one we

axle earth
between

one keeping
necks, another

keeping
sake &

pillar
fed

That thou forget'st so long

in knelt
number

argument
lay dwelt

song then
spent

into gates
whereby now

be made
silt, flame

slit, glade
& skill'd

Truth needs no color with this color fixed

color
neglects

silence
the

working
innocent

destruction,
it will

not
cling, suture

to me
the

sun, it
lies

&
trues

I lie awake like a lonely bird on the roof

i sometimes
hold

my tongue
turned

to the
prayer

of the
grass &

owl garment
so i

forget to
eat our—

all our
handiwork

days

selah

My bare invention quite, is more worth

so over
goes, so

to mend
dust w/

dust in
our

passenger
word, our

keeping
brief

castings, the
thieving

tune in
longer

turning, or the
beggar'd

blessing task
prefigured

'i had a
body'

'i had a
god'

land or
nod

blame me
not

Like the bloom of the field, thus bloom

so suture
muse

we bloom
&

mouth &
bloom

for—& don't
quote me

i won't
quote

So your sweet hue; hath motion
and June's burn'd beauty

there the ships go, pinion
gazelle, dial-hand

glowing fire, will you have
your habitation

light-crested, which yet
is green, is it, cloak

the sun knew its setting
& the winter knew—

stretch out your hand, he said,
be consumed out of

the earth, an innumerable
breathing, a spending into

voices, bandages, branches
constantly

And in this, a chance invention spent

but a few, & songs there
alike, fallen open

in a handful, a word
had come, tomorrow-kinding

'to one, of one, they chase
in the dry places,' year

like a river, they chase into
deer for, they spare or

spill the near dark, send
darkness, send nearness, spill

a continent & it grew
driftwood like a

worry-leaf, a living
i overheard

And for they looked, but with
divining eyes, eyes to wonder

of oxen
truth, quickly

they thrush-
lucked their

words
w/ broom w/

fire-glassing
swallow &

merriment,
merit

& mud, the
molten

wilderness
mends

of throat
of sweet

of grass
of brought

if lip
if

bright blue
lip

Their heart to labor, they fell

hand of the
doe

preoccupied
winter, pre-

occupied
dawn

gather the
uncertainties:

a crown
of

grasses
themselves

realms to
throat

yield
or calm,

away
leapt the

mortal
nuzzle

palms
out

Those who go down to the sea in ships, who do

& in nothing
every

wooden rib,
every working

nothing to
contain all

things,
waves,

self-stinging
brass,

a brindle
lungsack

(god)

Counting no thing old, thou mine, I thine

the tongue's
lower case

glory, i
thine

overtaking
brink, black

twines thru
two

fish w/
an

earth in
each

mouth
laced

swing

My heart is fixed, is fixed; My heart is lark, is lark

my holy
is

fixed, is
but fixed

is
but yet

grown,
pitches for-

ward & a
loom

drew
close

wiser

I am a prayer, that I give myself to pair

w/ my many
mouth, my

house, my
fasting flame

locust, the heart
in the midst

of the absence
cut, carpentry

best to the
hands, & to carry

off, i am
shaken, all

blamed

My heart is pierced, the earth is cut

breath

breast

breastbone

glassed

seemed

lead, lead

cut

cutting

dreams, the

stained

parcel, fore-

bled,

passerine

&

reft

This wide universe I call praise's mouth,
the mouth of silence

sun
deer

ox
love

give
mirth

rest
mouth

telling
some

way
wave

ring

Now all is done, have what shall have no end

from a brook
on the way

he drinks,
therefore he

lifts up his
head, shows

his neck to
make

a vulnerable
neck, thou

hast the dew
of thy

youth as a
wound, as

a wound on
the head, dear,

a nod to
bloom, the skin

to run coursing
overcame, thee,

i, a deer, its
skin as

merely tightened
air, a

tumbl'ng book

110 : 110

allayed, i

hear

Assure, I assure, eye

a wander-work
& the hands

are sure to
drink

patient-gown
to

cure the crier,
dyer, done

in both potion
& praise of

color, colours
color, colors

stumble
on sunlight

stun as i
bled thru

the shirt

So you o'er green and ariseth

& all-the-
world allow

grass glows
in-between

our bones
grow

an earth-
doll to

strive
countdown in-

to one
&

a tongue
keenly

spores to
lure

dissolve

O'er the sea, crow, o'er the night, dove

the sun
has

gone down
as the

same, as
the

same of
us, some

out of
bird, out

of
glacial

space, a
latch

or
set

pronounced
j as in

grass or
met

–allelu–

My most true mind thus maketh mine eye untrue

since i
left, barely

dust &
love

to bevel,
since

i lift sea
or

mountains
left

you,
heavens

i belong
incapable;

i spell
you &

i sparrow
you

barley &
below

Flint to a sun of water

green trembling
wrong, what

green trembling
wakes green;

at least the
crown wild

w/ green, that
i was

what i was i
taught to

still in green
& flee, o

trembling
crown, at least

found, gave
falling

Heavens are heavens for The Lord, and mouths, mouths

doubt not water
burns dearer

they have yet
hands, but

leaf not
throats

Whose millioned, my most full flame should afterwards

burst into
doubt, pines

into hands
the

earth walked
its

silence into
a

mouth, of
that i

am
certain

& a
crown

of
accidents, the

crown of
accidental

deciduous
minds

Or bend with the remover to remove

> return to
> error, calm
>
> i lift
> rest &
>
> sleeve,
> of needle
>
> i speak
> i
>
> return to
> believe

Delivers it out even to the edge, upon me proved

cup to
compass, it'll

brain my
viny saint, seed

& come to
sorrow-sight

tomorrow
we'll make

an error'd
mark

on my
forehead,

incite or
citation, the

incision

When in my days I called

the sun
for an

eye, the
moon for

an eye
lent—

a cloud
passes

prepares,
a deer

wills us,
our teeth

to
genuflect

Wherein I should repay, and given to time

call sail decisive,
forget

upon the frequent,
farthest; forest

every sail over-
whelms, all

tie me, day,
tied to

imminent
glacial

eyefold, the
keens &

waken'd
stations

to nook

Thus policy in love, to anticipate

fire-knock
then

thorn eager
answerer

either
shelter-cut

or feeding
gate

swarm me
sore &

soaring w/
seeding-breath

more
either &

the wide
open

opens

selah

Wondrous, I walked the straight line astray

to eat words, the earth is
filled, i saw

its end but not
words, i am

small, i dawned in
the morning like

a chosen morning
& went to

crying on your tongue,
let me see your

mouth's acre, hath my
heart the hidden

cedar—i am a
stranger in the

earth,
i am a stranger

How have mine eyes out of their spheres,
my mouth open wide

sun alms
or salt-

planet
entry, cape

or picket
bay, quickly

i distance
myself

out of
myself, very

this cloud
crushed to

glass or
pill, the

every
song

What can it add, a tongue?

that blossom
fits

a dwelling
fit to

juniper, the
pilgrim's

hammer,
this

torso'd
suitcase

unto weighs
burning w/

salve &
sewing

brass—in
mine taken

yours &
yours must

take me
in

For if I were, unless my nerves were

as i by
yours

i could
return

messages
"i am for

peace," but
when

i speak,
i hone

The sun does not strive you, nor the moon a tongue?

the mountain
cuffs & i

keep
frail-dealing

in my chest,
i line

& i
field w/

splattering
soil,

w/ shimmering
drift

a single
granite

drift &
w/ shimmering

row, fringe
on the

making lost,
making

toiled
coilspring

struck

Lost, *which is so deemed*

keep lost,
keep

your going
&

coming, your
frail

bevel, keep
your

slumber
blood, i will

not suffer,
i will

lift
into

Not by our being, but by others' seeing

i hold the
book so

you can
read thru

the window
at it; you

can't even
hold

the book
anymore

can't be
inside w/

it, it burns
to a yellow

mustard
flower—

turn the page,
please

like a
kingdom

May your lovers rest tranquil

let me
speak the

bruise of
moss

tranquilized
rock

to its
testimony,

it bleeds
a little

fog, tallies
eternity

together,
fables, for

in thy brain
thy

tables seek
thee, but

i, therefore

therefore

Let us go, let us two

a penny
antler

suggests

So our eyes wait upon, look to wait upon

that
she/they

have hands
have

haste have
watching

ever
heaven

handed
chase or

mercury dress'd
mercy

pressing—
haven't he

/they stars
a

charcoal
grip this

liminal
embrace

Which works th'inviting of short number'd hours

in our
necks, the

flowers
devastating

our needs,
the flowers

swallow, bloom
devastating

fills, the snare
was broken &

blooms the bird's
escape

falls,
grows over

Up past our necks then up past our necks

fortune
nor falls &

to follow
collar—

float up
to

fields
&

giving,
say

soul, say
little

green
grasping

say
lulls, say

grass

Time among time or time with time gathered

cut-out
coin collar

collar-song
this

tooth in
ought

mind's
moons

mine's
moons

the wind
aches

who was
for us

were it
not

Gazing spent, I bore the mountain sweet

> settle
> bend, a
>
> minute
> lain
>
> to take
> them
>
> off—
> thrive
>
> a canopy of
> hands
>
> like mountains
> dive the
>
> secret
> houses
>
> spent
> spelt

He walks along and weeps, the bearer of seeds,
the bearer of the seed bag, bearer of weeks

then will our
mouth fill w/

& our tongue
w/

sheaves that
by waning

grew, 'we
were

like them
that

dream'—
the sun

is a
seed, the

moon is
a seed, a

sovereign
speechless

to bleed &
keep

To build the house, to eat the bread

i am
breaking

breath, a
quiver, clever

sleep, ever
the watchhouse

w/ holy
borrowed face

counted
as if it

were clay to
eat of

clay, every
bower, steeple

every
leap

Tender inward of your motion, sweet fingers

key &
kiss a

jerusalem
vine

will be
well

w/ thee
poor

corner
socket

& whil'st
gentle

could
seclude

tending to
the

floorboard
telltale

gaits

No maker of sheaves, their embrace, their book

a'bliss in proof
the plowers plowed

they drew a long
furrow in my

back & felled it, 'by
which they

go & by which they
stay,' neither

sooner blessing
sooner, i bend so

to the wheat & its
swallowed lay, i

could want to
make an interlocking

rooftop w/
these hands

Were you to watch for wrongs and words,
and nothing like the sun

done to
snow

the morning
watchers

& my
being

nothing
like it

when i
walk

i will
upon

the ground
chase

out the
depths, see

the sun—
'it will

always
be wait

-ing, late,'
wake the

snow, then

Nor my soul even, nor my eyes, wondrous

closing sky, thy pitch-black
wondrous

& many suns
wondrous, i wait, stars

i blame a neck

bright, i
quiet

pilot, i knack
too

Nor that full star that ushers in the even

his forearm pocked w/ cherry blossoms,
her crown to bloom

surely my house to bud, bleeds, so
too, the lamp in the field of the

woods, swore truth to it—
swore beauty in the gleaming jar

here i will dwell, for i desired it,
many, the grass flows

around any obstruction, i will not
give sleep to my eyes

those eyes become
most & least, your face & haves

Whoever keeps me, let my harm be

as the
dew comes

down a
coming

down takes
a dew

upon the
mountain

takes to
fracturing

me this
thee

we come
down

Myself, I'll forfeit as that other mine

hands, have i lost
collected

lost hold, behold,
confessing lift w/ the

hand, through the hours
of the earth

through the hours
of the hand, i lost

all gill, i lost
night, i have

made every mercy
bind, made

an earth who
forsakes

To thy sweet will making addition thus and so ascend

who stand in the
ends of the

earth, the eyes
everyone, in the end

only a'change in
breath, all water

in the thread
shine

so are everyone's
seas, has

everyone's
mouth, meticulous

More than enough, your name

the water makes
breath &

sand spares,
the little

creatures
settle on my

body, the
equal sign

is calcium
white, this

time two.
ribs, love

The sea, all water, and yet receives

white

breaking

please

breaking

to

For nothing hold me, so it please thee hold

who soul, will soul
near the sea into wrists

levitate, the earth who pounds
will make a moon of—

make a flesh of it
who bread, will bleed

the sun to make
a breath to it, outstretch

who will so, mouthful
of circle, outpace the oaks

Beauty is, see where it lies, what hooks
hang my hearts, my hands

we hung
our

lyric, we
hid

in the
trees

in the
poplar

my heart
is

cunning, i
forget

may i
forget the

gasp-jaw
on

the weeping
fish

my right
hand to

river

selah

I do believe, I know, the age of hands,
the song of hands

love loves
habit

loves not
to

have, you
are

a jotter,
smaller

the bowl
to

worry the
beautiful

bowl to
words

w/in the
home

the visitation
the mouth

to receive
me, my

haven't

Age in words, therefore I lie with her

sing in
the

way you
age

stretch
out-day

your hand
i know

your forever
your

mouth
i habit

Dear heart forbear, the days were fashioned

the animal lies
down w/

its atom, not
a word

in my tongue
curious

lays upon my
heart

not one of
them

did lack
when i

counted, when
i darted

awake, when
i put my

handful of
earth to

its brow,
the

crux
of it, weighed

Though not to love, yet love to tell me so

list rain as an
accomplishment

list a bird tucked
in the lip

list sorrow, patience,
list spoons

list tongue-tied
lift, ill-wresting love

the people of the
tongue—why

i should grow
pressed fog

spills in the
valley

i should grow
hinges

Are you, to the sound

i lay
w/

the fog
laying

itself
in a

few
trees

a blue
hill, beside

an ever
bluer

mountain,
the straw

drawn
straight

dives

Do not press my tongue, but lend me words

skin on the
backbone

My uplifted hands as the evening, thieving

keys on my
eyes, to

you, my eyes,
a watch

on my mouth,
as one

cleavest my
mouth, as

one cutteth
wood upon

the earth,
upon

the
sweet

Errors note, but 'tis my part

who leaves unswayed
the likeness

perennial, the
expectant foliage

can't scribble out my
face, or the tongues

of concerned lichen's
impetuous

green—a thousand
slips of

rock by the
thousands

Root pines in thy heart, that when it grows

deer pour
out, & the

deserving
keep

a faint
rain, a

near speech,
a crown

of deer
w/

deer as
the

roots—in
the

roots where
you sing

your being
empty

into being
song, sing

into empty
until

empty

If thou dost seek to have what thou dost hide

> dearly
> beloved,
>
> the deer
> on its
>
> hind legs
> stretching
>
> little
> accidents
>
> up hind
> legs,
>
> gather
> together

My heart is desolate, embraces all living creatures

in the
morning

to you
i covered,

i covered
myself

w/ you,
catching

rain as
desperat'd

darkness,
blameless—

i need
not

eyes where
i am

going, once
the wince

of a
bell

And makes all swift dispatch

voyaging
mountain

press into
cloud—

mountain
creature

cough out
stream &

township,
blue enclosed

feed on
us

feed on
our

storm &
bring us

darkness to
shelter

us from
stars

Yet this shall I ne'er know, but live in doubt,
and deliver worshippers to a fallen tree

whose hand is,
become

a hand of
birds, their

songs, saplings
flown, tended

but being both
from me

'til fire, the
two-loves

i have, have
tilt

Let all creatures, let all sound, let all

anew all
breathed

close at
close should

day's eyes
follow-more

gentle,
hear hands

i gentle
hid

kind to
kindly i

let living
let

lip make
night, the

name opens
quite, rathers

to rescue
season &

tender-tell
say

you who w/
every

wondrous

next, you

& your
unsearchable

mouth
have

a way
always

Last saved my life, saying

"but because
you

salvaged me,
my love

forms only
from

you," she
said in

subtitle,
"let's have

a song
instead," he

replied

I will sing, while I have, while I go

he returns to her soil
she returns to his dust

the way we turn upside
down to feed, which feeds

on us, the center, the role
the having & earth

the knees, while i still a
lull, what feeds the selling

hours, is this the nod
is this the body, if hovers

You showeth your word, your word
runneth very swiftly, you call them

        scattered ones to gather
        fever-love, forth

        like ashes feeding
        everleft cures

        flourish now,
        grasses in the   ·

        wound, please,
        beyond number

        clouds or
        names.cover

        i have thought
        thee, or

        desire has no rest,
        please—

The sun itself sees not 'til, marvel

all the cedars
& the

eye, lest eyes
keep'st

(the sun itself, many
messages)

what eyes hath
put

in my head,
birds, o cunning,

& not so
true

fled, fledge
the earth, fulfill

When I forgot, am of myself, written

let me forget
eyes, call—

let me forget
mouths, myself

in your mouth, let
be in your mouth

gone in the
throat, the fawn

lowers, slows its
book of

defects: brindle,
partaken

or mistake adorns
the lowly

maker

Lute, lyre, ram's horn, timbrel, stringed
instrument, flute, and cymbal

let all that has
arbor, blur, thou

this becoming breathed
every, every ever

sway, let all that
skill-day, slight of

taught beloved, the
more i heard &

cause, bright beloved
sleeve, receive, let

all that have
null, let all

stay (aspen)
let

all that
tremble

Shall I go down by the mouth

hold it that i
call, kind of

my hands, kind
of a cuc-

koo, an anointing
annotation

bird, betray me
i do be-

betray two
notes falling

no farther
season, trees

praise,
cue

Yet who knows not conscience is born
of love, rises only to fall

i used to
feed, my

fingers form
the guitar;

the hands of
the wild

beasts, the
hand

of the lion
eats

out of my—
from

my hand

Their words for making, gather yourselves

a small
lost skin

a little
lost

sky, a break
in the

sky gave
eyes

beheld the
eyes,

the pure
hand, the

pure eyes
deliver

the pure
hand

spread out
when

i break,
how

distant

And to enlighten thee, gave eyes to blindness

deep break
of thy

deep broke
broken

song of
together

dwelling
bone or

Let me not, its leaves; lend me not, forget

i wake up
w/

leaves, i
dream

leaves,
i slept

& sleep
roots

set
fire to

water, even,
eye

love, borrow
cure-grew

follow for
or

cast

Life to keep, came, and by this, by that, I prove

in your living
every

living like
the sun

keeping
asleep, being

hands proves
the keeping—

the messenger
wears

a crown,
the crown

wears
a mouth

& the ends
of the light

of the earth
lean

on my
shelter (its

shoulder)

And the heavens will give their dew

torn two
pieces

by two
torn

accept the
vision

which speaks
of

you &
let

the stars
could

A Note on the Text

There are 154 Shakespearean sonnets and 150+ Biblical psalms (if you are willing to include the few extra-canonical "David Psalms" of differing final number, depending on your reference) to form an imperfect yet perfectly reasonable call and response. Every moment needs a diving board when one is trying to leap with a desirously leaping, continuously changing body, and perhaps a long collection is the place to test such a theory.

Numbers on the pages serve as a reference map to their origins, including some fortunate mishaps along the way. For this is what this book seeks: a journey of fortunate mishaps, as any good lover or saint has. Or perhaps, the relationship of texts as a stand-in for ever-widening, ever-coalescing living relationships.

Titles are often direct quotations, as are the very bodies themselves—except when they are not, as they are always fickle. As we are, they are porous, and we all slip through.

I take for my source texts *The Norton Shakespeare* (Editors: Greenblatt, Cohen, Howard, and Eisaman Maus, 1997) and Robert Alter's modern translation of *The Book of Psalms* (Norton, 2007), although occasionally a diversion to the 1611 King James Version must be excused.

Lastly, it must be admitted that one need not read a prayer book from beginning to end, or in one sitting, or at all times with scrutinized continuous intent. Repetitions instead form a ritual chorus toward which strangers may drift as necessary, in the lineage of making and unmaking traditions.

Todd Melicker regularly communes with the fog of the Outer Richmond of San Francisco. He is the author of the chapbooks *the immaculate autopsy* (Achiote Press) and *king & queen* (LRL Editions). *rendezvous*, his first full length collection, was published by Rescue Press in 2013 as the winner of the second annual Black Box Prize. His work can also be found in *VOLT*, *jubilat*, *Verse*, and *Tupelo Quarterly*.